Escape from the Green Recliner

A GUIDE TO AGING

Alia Sayegh, PhD, and Lois T. Wallen

To the wonderful offspring and amazing grands

CONTENTS

PREFACE

I am 82 and my friend is 81. We were sitting on her porch on a recent summer day recounting the ailments we and many of our friends had suffered. "Boring," I sang out. We both started to laugh.

But we realize that getting old is not funny, it's ridiculous.

So we decided to do something about it. First we're going to tell you exactly how we feel about what we've been through, to validate what you are feeling and let you know you have plenty of company.

Then we're going to list all the possible foibles facing us ancients, and what we have learned about ways to overcome them. Some ideas are mine, some are my friend's *(printed in italics),* but we more or less agree with each other on general principles. I am the general contractor of the book only because I get slightly less frustrated with my computer than my friend does.

But we start with paper and pencil, carrying both with us at all times in order to remember the ideas that surface occasionally. We tuck these items into wherever we keep our cell phones which should be with us 24/7 so we can jot down whatever it is that we thought of so we don't get ourselves crazier than we already are. Yes that is one sentence--let's not waste periods and use commas and semi-colons sparingly.

I.

Welcome to the "Golden Years"

1 HOW OLD IS OLD?

I just had a conversation with my hair stylist P., a very sharp and cheery gal, aged 50. Her salon, a local neighborhood shop, caters to many old people who toddle in on walkers, some with caretakers. I asked her if she ever gets tired of this endless parade of oldsters and she seemed surprised that I would ask. She explained that she really likes old people. I then asked her What is old? We batted that back and forth and decided that "old" is approximately 30 years older than whatever age we are at the present time. It's obvious, of course, that, by the time one reaches 70, the time span decreases and when we get to be 90, old is 91.

When I read the daily paper, I tend to focus on the obits. I've noticed that most of the dead are my age, give or take a few. The question naturally arises: how long are we going to live? My financial adviser informs me that I have enough money to last until I'm 94. So there's a number for a limit. Much of the small print in long-term health insurance contracts informs me that the policy is good until the age of 90. When I noticed that, I was glad I hadn't signed up for it.

I asked S., an independent woman in her fifties, what she

considered old age. "Around 80, I guess," she replied. She had come to visit her partner's parents. "You don't think about mortality until you have to deal with parents. Facing the reality of their decline is devastating to those of us who normally ignore old age. I think the older generation follows the doctors' dictates more placidly. We younger people count on computers first of all to understand our ailments. We argue with the doctors. We get several opinions. Older people seem to be more accepting of their decline and can get over-medicated."

I interviewed some young friends and neighbors to ask them "What is old?" They said more or less the same thing. They don't think of age in terms of chronological numbers but rather "I can't be specific because old age depends on attitude and physical health and ability." And then the jokes started. My companions were a 36-year-old businessman/entrepreneur, a 50-year-old computer technology executive, a 50-year-old gerontology physician, and a 54-year-old dentist.

You are an old man when you wear your socks mid-calf with shorts. You are an old man when you hike your trousers up above your waist. You are old when you wear a sweater in the summer.

You are old when you want to turn on the radio to hear "The Shadow."

You are old when you surf the channels looking for Lawrence Welk to find out what the top 10 music hits are.

You are old when you think Philadelphia still has two baseball teams and three newspapers.

For us folks already advanced in years, old age is not just in the mind. It resides in the body and is debilitating. You only have to walk through an assisted living facility to know this. It's a beautiful place with period mahogany furniture and has a name like Meadows or Fountains or something like that. You walk in and the first person you see lurches, the second hobbles and the third rolls in on a walker with wheels. You just want to run away and hang out with toddlers. It is a depressing environment. Psychologists who administer the Rorschach test to old people notice that they see hideous faces and monster masks in almost every ink blot. For the young, the world is full of promise and possibilities. With advanced age we find the world has contracted. There is a contradiction between the inward feeling that we are as we always have been and the outward proof (as we look in the mirror) that we have been transformed. We would like to cling to the illusion of perpetual youth, but we cannot.

Listen up, you Baby Boomers, aged 55-65, because you are in for a big surprise. AP polls show that Boomers look at aging with optimism. Many are quoted as saying that they don't care about wrinkles, just don't call them old. Are you kidding yourselves? By the time you get wrinkled, you are old, you silly children. Retirement can be great if you have other constructive ways to fill your time and the money to do what you want. It can also take away a purpose for life, a predictable schedule that can be comforting, and a means of taking your mind away from unpleasant stuff going on in your lives. It's a crap-shoot.

Technology to the Rescue?

Ray Kurzweil in his book "The Singularity is Now" writes of the time when biological man will merge with technology and we will be able to transcend the limits of our bodies and brains to live in a human world that extends beyond our biological roots. Technology builds on itself like any evolutionary process. Evolution created humans, humans created technology and now humans are working with increasingly advanced technology to create new generations of technology until machines will have progressed to be like humans and beyond. Robots the size of blood cells will be able to invade our bodies and cure ailments, thus extending our life expectancy beyond our wildest beliefs. This "singularity," the merger of biological man and machine, will occur sooner than one may think as these changes occur exponentially. We are talking in decades, not centuries. It will not affect us, the 81 and 82 year olds, but it will have real meaning for our offspring and their children.

In smaller ways, the nation is already beginning to grapple with the graying of the population, now referred to as the "silver tsunami." The size of the aging boom is staggering. By 2050, one in five Americans will be seniors, and worldwide, 400 million of them will be over 80. Articles are appearing in newspapers, television, and all other media about how to accommodate these aging "boomers." In cities like New York, where seniors will soon outnumber school children, there are plans to build more accessible housing, use idle school buses for senior transportation, and make sure traffic signals at busy intersections allow enough time for seniors to cross. There will be benches in bus shelters, grocery stores that deliver and offer single portions of fresh items, and public bathrooms with ramps. Most of these projects are being driven by non-profit and government programs, although some cities aim to get private businesses to ante up too.

Such work is getting a late start considering how long demographers have warned that the population is about to get a lot grayer. Don't you love the descriptions "grayer" and "silver" when so many of us have no idea what color our natural hair actually is now? I would love to read the label on the bottle to know what to call the color of my hair. Sable? Chocolate? Mahogany?

2 THE INDIGNITIES OF INFIRMITIES

The word "coward" comes from Middle English and is taken from an old French word, "couard." There are dozens of synonyms for it, all meaning ignoble fear in the face of danger or pain: chicken-heart, fraidy cat, faint of heart, lily-livered, yellow-belly, baby, mouse, milksop, craven, poltroon, recreant, and sissy, just for starters.

Not surprisingly, some of these adjectives very accurately describe how you feel as you age. You begin to engage in a constant battle for control over your feelings and actions. And it's not easy to redirect your impulses if they lead you astray. It was Goethe who said that he had to conquer himself anew every single day.

In her book "Coming of Age," Simone de Beauvoir quotes Proust: "Of all realities (old age) is perhaps that of which we retain a purely abstract notion longest in our lives." Then she goes on to talk about how aging was viewed throughout the centuries, ending with the study of gerontology. She studies how primitive societies deal with old folks. She discusses the power of money and class, and the sad fact that poor societies tend to leave their old people to die in order to promote the survival of the clan. Interesting, but no comfort there.

Old age means dealing with one indignity after another. The pain in my left knee, right hip and leg continues to plague me and to make it difficult for me to do the walking I need to keep fit. I am like the Little Mermaid from the enduring fairy tale of my childhood; when she cut off her tail to enable her to be with her beloved Prince, she suffered excruciating pain with every step. Then, I remember my heel spur and all my complaints about that. The spur was nothing compared to the broken, no the shattered ankle that followed. I survived that event with my husband's help. When he was suddenly no longer here I would awake in the middle of the night wondering who would take care of me. How would I manage?

The grandfather clock chimes eleven. I think of many old people I know. They take whatever medicine they're prescribed. Their tongues lap it up and they treat the side effects with another medicine and so, propped up by pharmaceutical discoveries, they go on and on. My body is so wedded to my mind that the thought of taking medicine indicates for me, a weakness. Why can't I learn to embrace the treatment, to fight the infirmities? I feel like a coward, fragile and timid.

I look at my calendar and see that except for physical therapy, it is mostly blank. I know that my mood lifts when I'm in the company of others, but here I am, alone and feeling sad. I see other widows have activities--Mahjongg, bridge - but I've been glued to the television and fear I am turning into a zombie. I hate my green leather recliner. I love my green leather recliner. It is my prison and my comfort. I head for it when I get home after a walk and revel in its comfort. I despise it when I sit in it too long and it becomes my cage and trap and morphs into a green and lonely cave. The television is ever-ready, the remote tucked conveniently between the cushion and the armrest. The newspaper is folded neatly on the little table nearby. One recreational device leads to another while I am glued to that green recliner.

3 GRAPPLING WITH GRIEF

Although the aging process brings a whole host of problems in and of itself, the most obvious and difficult challenge is dealing with the loss of friends and loves ones – each death adds another layer of grief and trepidation to your life. I lost both my husband and my son to cancer and pain of these losses was so raw and jagged it is indescribable.

In one way, my son's death is easier for me than for my daughter-in-law, because I still have the same friends, I am still going to the same places and doing the same things I've done for the past many years, so I'm not dealing with a "how am I going to get through today" sort of problem. On the other hand, I will never recover from this loss, so it's a hopeless thing and that's the way it is. This child was my DNA, my blood, similar physical characteristics, a piece of my own body. It's not a door slamming shut, it's an amputation. I will live with the reflected pain for the rest of my life.

Grief, we are told follows a neat and predictable process, the purpose of which is to reach "closure," a state where you close the door on painful things and move forward with life.

Unfortunately, it doesn't happen that way. You don't close grief away and you don't close fear away. The passage of time may wear down some of the sharp edges, but there is no such thing as "closure" in the sense of sealing it away in a place where you never have to deal with it again.

Some turn to their faith. Others lose it. I find solace in the words of others who have trudged down this path before me and put their feelings into the following wise and/or humorous words:

Anais Nin: Life shrinks or expands in proportion to one's courage.

W. Somerset Maugham: Life is too short to do anything for oneself that one can pay others to do for one.

Anton Chekhov: This too shall pass? Nothing passes.

If life was fair, Elvis would be alive and all his impersonators dead.

I'm not aging, I'm marinating.

God put me on earth to accomplish a certain number of things. Right now I'm so far behind I will never die.

Oscar Wilde: "I know everyone has to die, but I always thought that I would be the exception..."

As I mentioned before, I am a devoted reader of the obits, as thoughts of death and dying have hovered around the periphery of my mind ever since I turned eighty. Today four young people, from forty to sixty, two in their eighties and two in their middle nineties expired. Now those numbers are not of statistical significance, but they are interesting, nonetheless. They confirm the fact that death is not the exclusive province of the elderly even though we know that the majority of the dead over time prove to be old people.

I wondered what the ancients had to say about the topic. In the first book of the Old Testament, God was said to have looked out on all creation and "found it good." Some Biblical scholars interpreted this to mean that even the inevitability of death was good. Knowing that our days are numbered invests our deeds and choices with greater significance. Although the death of a loved one is excruciatingly painful, we can appreciate the fact that a world in which people die and new individuals are born offers the promise of renewal and improvement more than a world in which the original people live forever.

We also read in the Bible that after the expulsion from Eden, Adam and Eve were deprived of eternal life. Another Biblical scholar saw this as a gesture of grace on God's part, as they wouldn't have to live forever with the sad knowledge of what they had done wrong. There would be a new generation, offspring of Cain and Abel, born in innocence, to carry on.

It was only much later, at the end of the Biblical period, that the ultimate destiny of the individual was viewed as transcending death. Historically the shift occurred when Jews opted to die rather than give up their religion. If you are martyred for your faith, there must be some reward awaiting you. In heaven? There is not a hint of this suggestion in most of the Old Testament. The ancient Israelites believed that whatever ideal state they could achieve would happen within their lifetimes, and that death was final. The shift in philosophy towards a belief in some sort of afterlife carried over into other religions, from the Western version of heaven to the Eastern idea of reincarnation. These concepts can bring great comfort if you believe in them.

4 DEATH OF A SPOUSE

If you are a woman, the odds are that you'll outlive your spouse. If you are in your sixties when you suffer this trauma, you are still fodder for ravenous single men looking for a companion and/or caretaker. Facing a stranger across the table at dinner and trying to fill in awkward gaps in the conversation, you will be reminded of such times in your youth, except you are no longer young.

To be widowed in your late seventies or beyond presents the possibility of taking charge of your own finances and future. Over time you may begin to relish your independence, but in the beginning, the sheer weight of the responsibility can overwhelm you and leave you feeling extremely vulnerable. If your husband left things in good order, how fortunate you are. Even so, you are dazed to the point that certain tasks seem insurmountable, such as shifting titles (if your finances were separated for tax purposes) or changing ownership (if your accounts were in both your names). Everyone wants a proof of death and each time you present one of those documents it brings back waves of grief. In addition, every ache and pain seems predestined to the worst possible outcome, magnified because you no longer have someone by your side, watching out for you. You try to recognize your rawness compared to those whose loss was long ago and accept those feelings as a natural outcome of the process through which you are struggling.

When your spouse dies you come to terms with the idea that your life came to a complete stop. It's a door slammed shut that you can't go through and you have to turn away and go in another direction or you will be lost forever. You have to reinvent yourself.

Appreciate the fact that if you were lucky enough to have had a good relationship with your spouse, this end is going to suck. If it wasn't such a good relationship, it's a lot easier, but ask yourselves, Which would you have preferred?

Six months after becoming a widow, I began to look at our years together as a long chapter in my life--marriage, raising a family, being part of another person. Now I have to envision myself differently--as an independent person. It's a new chapter, hard because I am no longer young and my aches and pains remind me of my future demise.

One of my most difficult challenges was to forgive myself for the pain of following my spouse's end of life instructions. They were clearly stated--Do not intubate if he could not swallow. I had to respect his documented wishes. During one of the last days there was a surge in pressure in his brain, so they had to operate. He fought to keep the feeding tube from being forced down his throat, so eventually, after prolonged efforts, we withdrew food and hydration. I was sure that I was murdering my husband. Then there was the visit by hospice, the morphine. The examination to determine the pooling of blood on his body, and finally, a few minutes after he died--the sight of him. Not there. As though he molted his epidermis like a serpent, and left behind a dead skin, devoid of all that he was. Finally my feeling of relief and thankfulness that he was suffering no longer.

Now my feelings snap like a bungee cord between relief that my husband avoided all degradation, which he feared most of all, and my misery at the intense loneliness without him to share all the things we did together without thinking-- the walks, the shopping, the study of plants, and quiet sitting, but always together and in harmony. Every night I'd tell him, "Do you realize how lucky we are? Do you know how lonely it would be if we weren't together?" Now I know.

Joan Didion's writing helped me deal with the early days following my husband's death. The following quotes in particular captured my feelings precisely:

"Only survivors are truly left alone."

"Un seul etre vous manque et tout est depeuple." (One person is missing and the entire universe is empty.)

"We might expect, if the death is sudden, to feel shock. We do not expect this shock to be obliterative, dislocating to both body and mind. We do not expect to be literally crazy, cool customers. We imagine the worst days to be the earliest. We expect the funeral to be the worst. This is not the issue. The worst? The unending absence that follows, the void, the relentless succession of moments during which we will confront the experience of meaninglessness itself."

Montaigne's words of wisdom also helped me identify and

deal with my feelings, especially his essay on sadness. He talks of Psammenities, King of Egypt, who was conquered by the Persian King Cambyses. When the latter asked Psammenities why he did not cry when he saw his son being led to his death and his daughter degraded, and only cried when one of his soldiers died, he replied that the loss of the soldier was a grief that could be dignified with tears. The first two losses were so severe that they surpassed the power of expression.

Perhaps that is why I cry over a maudlin sad song or tale and remain stoic over thoughts of my husband's death.

II.

Coping Strategies

5 FAMILY AND FRIENDS

Well, now that we've aired out our feelings, we'll tell you about our strategies for coping with them. You will figure out as you go along that all the pitfalls we talk about we ourselves have stumbled over. If you take our sage advice, you might avoid some of them.

Let's start out by saying that friends can be your greatest support system, but only the right ones. Don't give up until you find the right ones and don't be dragged down by guilt when you have to give up the wrong ones. People's characteristics are exacerbated when they age. If they are needy or whiney or egocentric or manipulating when they were younger, believe me, they will be even more so when they get older. You may have been emotionally strong enough when you were younger to simply smile at this behavior while suppressing your mild annoyance. But believe me again, you will start to feel put upon and more than a little annoyed. Give them up.

We lose friends through death, so it's very hard to give up those we have left. You can separate yourself slowly, politely, and with compassion, but do it or you will become one of them.

Friendships are especially problematic after the death of a spouse. You try not to give up old friends, but you must be very careful not to fall into a hole trying to do this. You will have to learn to recognize that there are invitations you should avoid. Going out with your old crowd of couples may not be such a great idea. Inviting one couple to dinner, lunch or coffee can be ok, but if you start to feel uncomfortable, back off.

I've heard this from many single people, young and old, men and women. When they became single from either divorce or death, they did not feel completely comfortable socializing with their coupled friends and they gradually drifted away from those previously close associations. Some felt abandoned by those friends. Some, as I did, no longer felt that we lived in the same circle of society and that we should take it upon ourselves to seek out other single friends with whom we shared a similar lifestyle. There are still several couples with whom I socialize but more often than not, I meet these women, the distaff side of the couple, for lunch or meetings or other women's activities. This is ok, people. This is the culture that we live in. Accept change without resentment and adapt to it.

If you go out with a couple or several couples, firmly and graciously insist on paying your share. If the gentleman is adamant, accept it and make it clear that it's a one-shot deal and next time you must contribute. Don't sit on your hands when the check comes. Try putting a $20 bill on the table and saying it's for the server. Have the money unobtrusively in your pocket so you don't have to root around in your pocketbook for it.

If you expect to be invited, you must also extend invitations, whether it's a group of women friends, mixed sexes, or any combination thereof. Take-out is fine. Who doesn't love pizza? On your birthday invite people to a modest restaurant and make sure when you go in (or call in advance) that the server discretely puts the check in your hands after dinner. Here's a short lesson in a foreign language: Don't be a "schnorrer." (For those of you who did not have a Yiddish grandmother, Google it.)

Surround yourself with young 'uns. You can never have enough kids in their 40's and 50's. They have fully developed frontal lobes and have already sowed whatever wild oats they had. They can be bright, funny and often parentless. We have "adopted" our neighbors, (M., C., and R.), and our sweet and lovely Pilates instructor (C.), who thinks we're the cat's meow because we can move our arms and legs. Hopefully, your own biological children will not be jealous and will gladly share you. They will, as ours do, enjoy all those extra "sibs" and be relieved that these treasured children will be helping to check on you, making sure you show yourselves at some time during the day to prove that you did not fall down the steps in the middle of the night.

As for your own children, appreciate their love and draw sustenance from it. The nicest birthday present I can ever remember getting was a card from my daughter, on my 80th birthday. It showed a picture of an adorable orangutan with a huge bunch of bananas stuffed in its mouth and had a caption that read: TO HELL WITH MODERATION. Well, that's not exactly what we are preaching here but the note inside is worth keeping. She said "Dear Mom: You have been an inspiration to me all of my life, but particularly in recent years. You are strong, brave, adventurous, and you know how to have fun. You never get tired of learning new things and meeting new people, which makes you the youngest 80 year old I know. You are a great friend and I love you."

I don't always feel strong and brave, but this inspires me to try harder.

Most importantly, remember that your social life is constantly evolving, and the best thing you can do is roll with these changes. The monthly dinners with 7 friends will diminish, then cease as one, then two, then three friends develop problems that preclude their participation. The pleasant early Sunday morning breakfasts will fade out for one reason or another. Their shelf life runs past the "sell-by" date. Just as art is constantly evolving, from Impressionism to Expressionism to Cubism to Abstraction, our social lives keep changing. Exchange the old routines for new ones, but don't mourn their passing. You enjoyed the experiences? Good, now move along.

6 BOOKS AND OTHER ENTERTAINMENT

Many seek enlightenment in religion, and for some it undoubtedly helps, but be wary of that daily Bible reading. You don't want to get into too much of that smiting stuff. You could get carried away walking on the sidewalk muttering, "I shall smite thee if that is thine own dog besmirching my newly cleansed lawn. You must now take your blue plastic newspaper bag and purify my dwelling." If the person is small and older than you, you could add "you heathen, you."

Travel Books? Don't bother because you've probably already been there two or three times and can tell them things like that "room with a view" is twenty-five miles out of town or yes, take the donkey ride to the top but skip the tram ride around the artichoke plantation. It's hokey.

Dummies books are excellent. Good, common sense information and nobody is trying to make you believe they're a genuine accredited psychologist. This is very different from the "how-to" book written by someone who took Psych 1 in freshman year. They are more likely to make you feel guilty if you don't agree with them, whereas Dummies books give you the leeway to say, "Aw, you're nuts."

Forget about romance novels. If you don't have a "torn bodice," it will make you jealous. Detective stories, on the other hand, are good. Make sure they take place in England or Italy. Be wary of the American ones unless you need a graphic description of what the head and surrounding floor and walls look like after the victim has been bashed in with the ubiquitous "heavy, blunt instrument." Also make sure the detective is tall and well-built or thin and nice looking but not too handsome. My apologies to Detective Salvatore Guarnacci (series by Magdalen Nabb) who will always be my favorite in spite of what I just wrote.

TV and movies: The same formula as above applies. Don't be fooled into thinking there is something wrong with the way you look because the women in the real world do not look like those gorgeous creatures portrayed as detectives, forensic scientists, doctors, lawyers, etc. Hello! They live in Hollywood, guys. You would not really find them in police stations, labs, hospitals and courtrooms. The people in those places look like you and me. See Topic about Appearances.

Music: It seemed for a while as though the Big Band music you so fondly remember from your youth was disappearing from the radio. According to the radio trade publications, nobody wanted to be identified with songs referred to as "oldies," thereby eroding financial support for the stations that played them. Then, a few years back, satellite radio became widely available, with specific channels devoted to entire decades, from the 40's on up. Alternatively, you can always find Bach, Brahms, and other really old dead guys on commercial radio. Their appeal cuts across generations, and they'll make you feel young by comparison.

7 THE DAILY ROUTINE

At first I resented the repetitive tasks of living alone. I went about the business of opening all the blinds in the morning and then closing each one carefully, in the dark, every night. Now I am grateful for all the demands the house makes on me. It binds me to life. Repaint the trim. Prune the plants. Repair the brick. Better than having someone wait on me, spoon-feed me, take care of everything for me.

<u>When to call in the pros</u>

If you are living alone after many years of being a family and you had a division of labor, like he did the laundry and you did the checkbook, you will learn many new skills. You will learn to take care of some things yourself for the first time, and you will learn when to call in a professional. Here is a list of those you may need:

- *an accountant and/or financial adviser (not necessarily the same one)*
- *a lawyer*
- *a mechanic*

- a *carpenter*
- a *plumber*
- a *podiatrist* or *pedicurist (Don't tell me you can still bend your foot up to your eyes to cut your nails.)*
- *an electrician*
- *the usual array* of *doctors, chiropractors, acupuncturists, etc.*
- a *cleaning service because you have mopped up enough floors to last a lifetime*
- *someone to cut the lawn if you have a lawn (Put the mower out by the curb and someone will come in the night to get it.)*

You will learn to deal with each of these people as required. To your new friend, the gas station guy, be honest. "I don't know Jack Sprat about a car except how to drive one, so I am putting myself in your hands. I am going to trust you. If it comes to pass that you are screwing with me, I will go to the gym and find someone to beat you up."

"Listen up Mr. Carpenter, I do not want a curtain on this new shower stall that you built, I want a glass door. Yes, there is room for one. I know it's a bit narrow, but I do not weigh 400 pounds. I will suck in my breath if need be, all the while withholding payment of your bill until I get what I want."

"Yes, good morning to you too Mr. Plumber. I know I called you on a weekend, but $500?"

How do you find these people? Ask your friends, neighbors, the lady who does your hair, or go to the computer. Don't bother with the telephone book because even Superman can't read it without his contact lenses and a magnifying glass.

Having said all that, you don't have to call a handyman to change a light bulb, insert screens or undo a screw if you remember these words to turn anything off or on: "Righty tighty, lefty loosey." Your tools on hand should include large and small Philips-head screw drivers, large and small regular screw drivers, ice pick, needle-nosed pliers, small wrench about 9" and not too heavy, and small, light-weight hammer, also about 9." If you need a heavy duty tool, you need a professional – don't mess with anything that will break your toe if you drop it.

Speaking of screwing in gadgets, don't do your own smoke detector alarms. Call the fire department to install them and have them come back to change the batteries once a year. I call every January 1ˢᵗ because it's easy to remember. They will welcome your call. What they really don't like is carrying your dead weight out when you have a fire and no smoke alarm. If you set the kitchen one off because the oil in the pan is smoking but there is no fire, take the pan off the stove and put it in the sink on a trivet. Wave a towel back and forth under the smoke detector and open the window. Whatever else you do, do NOT climb on a chair to stop it unless someone very very strong is holding on to your legs to steady you. And speaking of alarms:
The stove takes no paper
The microwave no metal.
You want your tea?
Use the stove for the kettle.

Remember that tea bags often have tiny metal staples in them and that scalding water boiled in a microwave in a narrow cup can suddenly bubble up over the edge of the cup. Use a kettle with a loud whistle, set the timer and carry it with you in your pocket when you use a burner to cook.

Speaking of pockets, are aprons not fashionable? Who cares! A bib apron or smock with copious pockets will hold the timer, cell phone, glasses, keys and maybe an apple and a banana.

Speaking of aprons, they control "age spots." Not the ones on your skin, silly, the ones on the front of your shirt – men's on the stomach and women's on the bosom. Kids get stains on their shirt fronts, teens get them, 40-year-olds get them, so why do they laugh at us and call them "age spots"? Do they think we can't see them? Do they think we don't care? Do they think we dribble our food?

Ok, back to tips for easing your way through the daily grind. If the local gas station is a few blocks from your house and the dealer is 6 or 8 miles out on the highway, it's easier to pay a little more and go "local" for car service. He runs a small operation paying "city" rent but your car won't be tied up for a whole day or more and it's easily accessible when it's finished.

By the same token, if there are two comparable restaurants that you enjoy and one has a large parking lot and the other none, are you going to drive around and around the block looking for a spot? Don't be silly.

Nor does it make much sense to buy in bulk anymore from those wholesale clubs. You don't need a 20-pound box of Tide, and the effort of hauling it through the front door isn't worth the savings.

Another way to make your life easier is to "de-clutter." Remember that your heirs will not only get your money, but they will also inherit every piece of junk, all your collections, photographs in duplicate and triplicate, old clothing that you don't wear anymore - I can go on and on. Start now to cull through your things. Clean out your drawers, closets, and kitchen cabinets and throw away all of those empty peanut butter jars that you think will be useful some day. You will feel better without the clutter and your heirs will thank you, even though you won't be around to hear them say it.

Staying Busy

One thing you do want to clutter up is your calendar. Staying busy distracts you and keeps you from dwelling on the negative. Fill up your days with activities like museum visits and other outings. There are free film series at local libraries, concerts in parks, and craft shows at community centers. Just getting out of the house can lift your spirits - use the library reading room instead of your recliner.

I must add that keeping busy does not mean that you need to be with friends and family every minute of the day. There are times when it's actually good to be alone. But first you have to rid yourself of obsolete feelings that tend to invade your psyche. I often considered being alone a bad thing, particularly after my husband died. But as time went on it seemed to me that my feelings about loneliness belonged to the distant past. Did I first feel alone when a friend of my parents left me locked in his car for a long time while he stopped to see a patient instead of delivering me directly to my house? Did they start when I came home from school to a baby sitter who pinched me when I didn't do her bidding and I sat sulking in my room? Did they begin when a boyfriend didn't call and I sat dejected by the phone feeling abandoned? It doesn't matter which of these events triggered feelings of abandonment and loneliness. When I analyze my feelings today I realize that I rather enjoy being alone in between the scheduled outings. It is important not to let atrophied emotions impinge upon current day realities. Learn to filter out those ancient emotions and to substitute your real feelings.

One more thought on this: if you don't like being alone, but you don't necessarily want people in your house morning, noon and night, I've got a great solution. Get a dog. They're great company and keep you so occupied you don't have time to mope around. They act like small people except you can go out, close the front door and leave them alone in the house. Just because you are not paying a babysitter, don't think they come cheap though. Vet's fees are definitely not covered by the Medicare you have grown so used to, but on the other hand, a huge bag of Kibble will feed a small poodle for half of forever. I suggest that the older you are, the older the dog should be. When you waddle, they will waddle. A young dog will want to run and running is murder on old knees. Just remember that old dogs need the same kind of care that we do – they get arthritis, tooth and gum disease, and finally, senility. But a dog will love you unconditionally; they feel soft and fuzzy, and you can talk out loud without seeming to be crazy. People will think you are talking to the dog. You can, of course, stick a Blue Tooth in your ear and accomplish the same trick.

8 FOOD AND COOKING

When it comes to cooking, I have some simple advice: Wean yourself away from customs that are no longer relevant to your current life. You don't need to make those huge meals for the family served on Rosenthal china plates alongside sterling forks and knives. This shift may happen gradually over a period of time. First you may reduce the stemmed wine and water glasses to just one of the two. Then you'll be serving hors d'oeuvres on paper plates with plastic forks and knives. Eventually you'll realize that dessert deserves the same fate.

I have found that in addition to going casual, it also helps to be very organized. I prepare a menu, go grocery shopping two days in advance, and set my table a day ahead, taking out every pot, pan, dish and serving piece that will be used. My actual cooking can be done last-minute, but even the un-refrigerated ingredients like salt, pepper, spices, jars, etc. that I'll need are on the counter the day before with all of the utensils.

I'll then take the menu that I printed on my computer, snip the items separately and put the scraps of paper inside the serving dishes where they will go, along with the appropriate serving pieces. This entire calculated schedule serves three purposes:

1. *Doing the physical activity does not tire me out because it's spread out over a time period.*
2. *It's easy for guests who come into the kitchen to help because it's all "spelled out."*
3. *We O.C. people love organization. I'll organize a box of toothpicks if I don't stop myself.*

My writing partner is particularly good at advance planning. When we arrive for dinner at her house, the buffet is fully loaded with hot plates lined up and every morsel prepared and covered with aluminum foil. She will then leisurely sit down with us in the living room looking for all the world as though she hasn't done a lick of work. However, not all of us need this kind of organization to feed a crowd. J. does her delicious, healthy dinners last minute. After raising five kids, she doesn't rattle easily.

But whether I'm feeding a crowd or just myself, I no longer scour my cookbooks for exotic recipes that take hours to prepare. If I want that kind of food, I bring my own booze to a nearby restaurant and recommend that they put that yummy looking braised deer antlers smothered in kiwi flavored raisin sauce on their menu. For my everyday meals, I've made three new friends, Amy, Joe and Annie. Here is sample dinner for you: You will need one microwave oven, a sharp knife to slit the paper and two oven mitts so you don't burn your hands, along with the following:

1. *A package of Amy's organic whatever (the vegetarian lasagna is tasty)*
2. *A bag of Trader Joe's pre-washed salad*

3. *A bottle of Annie's organic salad dressing.*
4. *Optional--a bottle of Yellow Tail merlot and for sure a chunk of chocolate bark.*

Quotes on food preparation:

I love cooking with wine and sometimes I even put it in the food.

I like cats too. Let's exchange recipes.

Red meat is not bad for you. Fuzzy green meat is bad for you.

Nutrition is very important for old people and if you are reading this, you are probably old, so I'll keep it simple. There are five basic food groups: red wine, dark chocolate, coffee, oily small fishes (only wild and not farmed) and --here you get to pick one--spinach, broccoli and/or dark green lettuce. If you opt for something more exotic like kale, that would be cooked like escargot disguised with about 20 cloves of garlic. It's okay to eat 20 cloves of garlic because old people lose their sense of smell along with their bone density.

We speak of memory and hearing loss in another section but in the meantime, repeat after me: anti-oxidant, Omega 3, anti-oxidant, Omega 3, anti-oxidant, Omega 3. Very good!

Finally, I must extol the virtues of eating out as opposed to eating in. For one thing, if you don't have a load of ingredients in the house like you used to, by the time you get through buying the components of a whole meal, it can sometimes be cheaper to eat it in a restaurant. And speaking of restaurants, we love those early birds. Don't be embarrassed because you eat dinner at 4:00 PM. Tell anyone who kids you that it's your lunch and you eat dinner European style at 10:00 PM. You don't have to tell them that the values are great, you don't drive after dark and you go to bed at 9:00 PM.

There is another advantage. There is no longer any such thing as a lovely, peaceful, quiet dinner in a restaurant. Just like the doctors' waiting rooms, there must be "background" music and as the earlier diners talk to be heard over the music, each subsequent table of diners will talk even louder to be heard over the music, over the other diners. Get the picture? The later the hour, the more the customers come in and the worse the cacophony. It's relatively peaceful at 4:00 PM.

9 SAFETY FIRST

You have to be careful about your safety as you never were before. You are alone. Notice the bulge in the carpet and make a mental note to step over it. Don't turn off the light in the den before you walk over to turn on the hall light, even though you know you'll have to walk back to the den to put out the light you were reading by. Don't ever wander around in the dark. Besides, the extra walking poses no problem. In fact it is good for you.

Falling is to be avoided at all costs. Yet, obstacles will pop up when least expected. Returning from depositing the recycling in the bin, I was walking through the almost empty garage when I tripped over a plastic bag filled with my husband's landscape plans. It was peeking out just a few inches from the box that held the rest of the plans. Before I knew it, I was down on my knees, those poor knees that could barely survive another shock. They are the very knees I've been nursing along with acupuncture to avoid replacements. That's the nature of an accident. It just happens. Like that. In a millisecond. Still I was able to get up. Pure luck! Or was it due to the almost daily exercises? Ice was my salvation--twenty minutes on, twenty minutes off for the first two days. How to avoid the surprise obstacle? Double vigilance. My son told me the solution was to lay mattresses over the floor of every room and to roll over and over on them to get from place to place.

Forget about Crunches: article by Jane Brody in the New York Times of June 28th, 2011.

"It's too easy to suffer a vertebral fracture - a compression, or crushing, of the front of a vertebra, one of 33 bones that form the spinal column. This injury is very common, affecting a quarter of postmenopausal women and accounting for half of the 1.5 million fractures due to bone loss that occur each year in the United States. Men over age 60, many of whom suffer them, are unaware of the problem and receive no treatment to prevent future fractures. By age 80, two in every five women have had one or more vertebral fractures, often resulting in a hunched posture, a condition called Kyphosis. If a vertebral fracture is diagnosed and properly treated, the risk of future fractures, including hip fractures, is reduced by half or more, studies have shown."

Some guidelines recommended in the medical journal Osteoporosis International suggest exercises to improve posture, strengthen back muscles and enhance mobility, along with dietary supplements (organic only), proper nutrition and awareness. Bend safely from the hips and knees, not the waist. Do not twist; turn to face the object you wish to reach before you bend and avoid overreaching. Don't reach for objects on a shelf higher than one you can touch with both hands together. Protect your back when you cough or sneeze by tightening your abdominal muscles and support your back by leaning against a wall.

Get a dexascan to determine bone loss, note whatever your doctor recommends and then be your own advocate. Get on the computer, check out the meds and then ask your doctor about adverse side effects, whether it's an immediate reaction or a possible counter-productive effect after one or two or even three years. A good, concerned doctor should welcome this discussion. By the way, make an appointment to talk to him or her with your clear, concise questions written down and be considerate of his or her time.

Make sure this doctor is aware of any and all medications you are taking. Write them all down so you don't omit anything. Over-medicating can be dangerous, and/or dull your mind.

Traps are lurking all around us unnoticed: the door closing on the vulnerable toe, the bag of blocks left over from the grands peeking out to trip us on the way to the powder room, inhaling the crumb of an innocent piece of toast so that it enters the windpipe and causes endless spasms of choking. All these mishaps can occur within a half hour of each other. Yes, eating takes special concentration. The old admonition of chewing your food carefully takes on new meaning. You had better take it slowly or you could choke to death.

Speaking of food, remember the snow pea. The snow pea? It sounds innocent enough. Yet I had a dinner companion who started choking on one of these in her salad. It scared her, scared me and scared the server. Ever since, she and I peel off the strings and then eat the pea with caution. I dare say the server still looks at snow peas with trepidation.

Along with food concerns, beware also the last three steps of any staircase. Sneakers can be sneaky with their wide heel and grabbing rubber bottoms. Always keep one hand on the railing, and throw down to the bottom of the stairs anything in that hand. Avoid throwing glassware, children or food. You know the drill. When faced by a public staircase, grab that railing right down to the bottom step even if it's disgusting. You can scrape the chewing gum off your hand when you get to the bottom and wash off the bubonic plague germs in the ladies'.

A few more words on our fragile bones: walk like a prancing horse. Lift your feet off the ground and place them heel toe, heel toe. Don't drag or scuff them. Unless you're walking on ice. Then you slide each foot along without picking it up at all. (More about ice and snow later.)

The most important rule of thumb when you're taking care of yourself is to listen to your own body. Ten months after my husband died, I was sick, exhausted from a fever, and wanted nothing more than to lie in bed. However, I decided I had to get up and stretch my bad right hip. I put left foot over right, hands on hip and bent to the left in a deep stretch. I went down. My hip broke. By a wild stroke of luck my cell phone was nearby and it saved me. I could reach it from where I lay. I don't know anyone's number by heart, because naturally, they are programmed into the phone. A call to a friend to tell him where the hidden key was located saved my front door from being bludgeoned. Afterwards, there was the hospital, surgery, rehab, outpatient physical therapy. Every step was agonizing. The challenge was to keep my spirits up and to persevere doggedly with therapy and the grueling work of rehab. I kept asking myself whether it was worth doing all this work for another brief stretch. The alternative was to revert to helplessness. Nope. I knew I had to muscle my way through, hoping for improvement, measuring each incremental gain.

10 THE WEATHER

Everyone talks about the weather, but nobody does anything about it. Wouldn't it be lovely if we could? We would arrange to have rain between 2:00 and 4:00 a.m. when most of us are sleeping. The temperatures would not go below 55 nor above 75 and if we wanted snow, we'd run up to Canada or, better yet, over to Switzerland. In the real world, however, we must deal with what we do have, which is snow, ice and the sun peeking through the ozone layer.

We know that you know how to navigate through snow if you must, but try not to. Heed the reports and arrange to fill your house with all of the necessary things you will need if you get house-bound for several days, including fresh batteries and flashlights placed in several strategic, accessible places throughout your house or apartment. Make sure your cell phone is charged and in your pocket and don't be shy about calling 911 if you get into trouble. They would prefer to help you while you are alive and kicking instead of out cold on the floor when the electricity goes out, the heat goes out and your nerves give out.

"Black Ice" is the devil in disguise. It really is almost invisible, so make sure you are clutching the railing with both hands when you step outside for the morning paper. It would be so

embarrassing to go flat on your bum dressed in your nightie. I save the wooden rollers from discarded, torn window shades because they have those little metal prongs on each end and if you use them as walking stocks, they grip into ice while they're giving you balance. By the way, if you don't have a railing outside, GET ONE and get a professional to install it so it doesn't wobble. It's a necessary expense – put off the yacht until next year.

A word about hurricanes and other fierce weather: those of us who grew up at seaside resorts have a peculiar habit of going down to the ocean to watch the action at the height of a storm. We are aware that this is a really dumb idea, so do as we say, not as we do. And leave us alone with what may seem to you like a death wish, but is only a slightly defective gene. Get thee to a safe place and stay there.

There are three things to remember about heat, besides the fact that it can kill you.
1. *brimmed hat*
2. *plenty of water to drink*
3. *sunscreen #30*

Keep yourself hydrated. Even if you prefer Scotch to water, drink the water.

11 MEDICAL ISSUES

We will start this section noting that none of our healthcare information is to be taken as professional medical advice – you need your own doctors for that. But we pass it along because it seems like interesting, useful common-sense guidance.

The Senses

Hearing loss is one of the many indignities that accompany old age. Don't be coy. Instead, say in a loud, clear voice, "If you want a conversation with me, look me in the face. No, no! Don't turn your head away to look at the scenery. Speak up, speak up distinctly, preferably in English. Modulate your voice, which means don't squeak and for heaven's sake, don't whisper. That is so annoying." If, after that piece of advice, they shout at you, you may say something polite like, "Hey stupid, keep it down to a roar! Do you see me with a trumpet in my ear like Beethoven? Well, do you?"

The eyes will also fail you, but here there's actually something you can do about it. Don't be afraid of cataract surgery. Well, OK, be afraid, but do it anyway. If you put it off until you can no longer drive after 4:00 P. M. you learn to live like that.

When you do get your eyes back, that habit can get ingrained in your brain. If, however, you are nervous and jerky about driving under whatever conditions seem to make you nervous and jerky, then don't do it unless you carry a lot of insurance and can afford to keep buying new cars. Sorry, we have no advice on old people's diminished reflexes. Well, actually we do, but that's in another section.

By the way, the surgery is a piece of cake. They stick something in your vein that is so cool, you don't care what they do. And it's legal. Incidentally, when we enter the doctor's office, do we really need that T.V. blaring in every waiting room? Do doctors really think that we won't get angry when we are kept waiting for an hour if we are entertained by the loud T.V.? Don't be shy about explaining this to your doctor. Do it before your examination or after. You will not be taken seriously while you are clad in only in a paper gown and your socks.

Memories – or Lack Thereof

It's almost a dichotomy that the older we get, the more we forget things and the older we get, the more we know things. We forget where we put the keys or whether we paid the electric bill. "Hey, I could have sworn I just put those keys in my pants pocket! Where did I leave them?" Conversely, I remember an electric storm in the 1940's in which A.'s companion was struck and killed by lightening; I never forget to get out of harm's way when I hear thunder. We live on a barrier island and I lost my Oldsmobile to floodwaters in the 1966 hurricane. I never forget to move my present car to high ground when I see that swirling circle coming up the coast on the weather map. Does this mean that our subconscious mind differentiates between danger and annoyance?

43

The good news is, aging doesn't automatically imply a progressive loss of mental and neurological function. Recent science suggests that the brain is able to change physiologically, creating new neurons. The bad news is, between the ages of 80 and 85, 1 out of 4 people will have some degree of dementia, and after age ninety, 99-100%. Today, the biggest worry among people 55 years old and up is not the Big C, but the Big A, Alzheimer's.

Assuming that some memory loss is inevitable, there are little tricks you can employ to deal with it. For example, when you see your children roll their eyes as you launch into a story, it probably means "I can't believe she's (he's) going to tell me that story for the 100th time" or "Good grief, she (he) just said that not 3 minutes ago. Gimme a break please." Try a quick recovery like "Oh, I forgot when I mentioned this 3 minutes ago, there's another part I didn't tell you." Then say "Oh, never mind, it's not really important." Another strategy might be to assume you already told that story and try a fishing expedition. "You remember my telling you about how Grandmom used to eat ice cream with catsup and parsley on it?" If they say yes, carry on with "She also put roasted potatoes on it. Ha, ha."

Compulsive habits will come in handy in preventing constant misplacement of keys, phone, wallet and other essentials. Put your pocketbook in the same place and toss your keys in the little china dish by the door. If you need reading glasses, rush to your nearest pharmacy and buy at least five pairs of the commercial variety, place them at conspicuous spots around the house, and revel in their profusion. (It's not a bad idea to invest in a magnifying glass for the small print on the medicine bottles either.)

When you suddenly remember something you want to

remember, repeat it out loud. I climb the stairs shouting the entire time I'm climbing, "Empty the hamper, empty the hamper, empty the hamper." Of course, I do live alone so I don't scare anyone during this process. I do something similar if I'm introduced to someone I'm likely to run into again (but in this case I keep it inside my head): "The man's name is Edgar Dimmwitt, Edgar Dimmwitt, Edgar Dimmwitt."

I also recommend keeping a calendar that you check every morning and night, and making shopping lists that you keep in an accessible place in the kitchen or on your desk.

Some studies suggest that you can do more than simply learn to cope with memory loss. For example, we all know that smoking will rot your lungs, obesity will stop your heart, cholesterol will clog your arteries, high blood sugar will put in you a coma and high blood pressure will finish the job. But did you know that all of the above will shrink your brain in an area known as the hippocampus? A recent study by researchers from the University of California Davis evaluated data on 1,352 people whose average age was 54. The data, generated from the Framingham Offspring Study that began in 1971, suggested that the onset of mental decline may be speeded up by as much as a decade in participants with the risk factors I just mentioned.

According to an article from Health Realizations, Inc., sent to us by Dr. James Gaeta's Family Health Centers in Marlton, NJ, some memory loss is short-term and can be traced to very specific incidents:

- Head injuries
- Medication – more likely to cause memory loss among the senior population, where it's not unusual to be

45

taking many prescriptions simultaneously described by different specialists

- *Antacid – one study published in the Journal of the American Geriatric Society even found that elderly African Americans who regularly use antacids have nearly 2.5 times the risk of developing dementia*
- *A lack of protein or inability to digest it properly – fortunately, fulfilling your daily requirements of 70 grams of protein a day is relatively easy: a bowl of cereal, a peanut butter and jelly sandwich, a piece of fish or chicken and a side dish of legumes meets the protein requirements for the day for an average adult*

Saving your Life with a "Hearty" Cough

Everyone should know what to do in case they suffer a heart attack. At our age, it will very likely happen when you are alone. You can help yourself by coughing repeatedly and very vigorously. A deep breath should be taken before each cough, and the cough must be deep and prolonged, as when producing sputum from deep inside the chest.

A breath and a cough must be repeated about every two seconds without let-up until help arrives, or until the heart is felt to be beating normally again. Deep breaths get oxygen into the lungs and coughing movements squeeze the heart and keep the blood circulating.

Dangers of Drugs (Not the Kind on the Street)

We used to worry about protecting our children from the dangers of drug poisoning, but the elderly need to worry just as much. The Maryland Poison Center collected data from the American Association of Poison Centers that showed that adults age 40 and older account for 16% of poison exposure calls to the nation's 57 poison centers but they make up 56% of deaths from poisoning. The calls came from adults who took too much of their medicine, took someone else's medicine or are concerned about a drug interaction. Here's some advice from the Poison Center:

1. *Know about each medicine you take (name, color, markings, dosage, etc.).*
2. *Read the label to make sure you are taking the right dose.*
3. *Follow the instructions to take your medicine the right way. Some medicines interact with food or alcohol, and some should not be taken with other medicines.*
4. *Keep a list of all your medications and share the list with your doctor at each visit.*
5. *If more than one doctor prescribes medicine for you, talk to each doctor and your pharmacist so they can check for drug interactions.*
6. *Never take someone else's medicine.*
7. *Put on your glasses and turn on the lights before taking medicine, especially at night.*
8. *Talk to your doctor before you take a natural or herbal supplement.*

Mistakes can be made at the most reputable pharmacies. Customer lines can get crowded, pharmacists can get distracted, staff can be shorthanded. Anyone can make a mistake. Make sure you know the name of the medicine prescribed before you go in so that you know the correct name and what the dose should be. If you can't read the prescription, ask the pharmacist what it is when you order it. When you receive your purchase, open the bag at the counter or before you leave the store and make sure that it's your name on the bottle, that it's the medicine you ordered, and that the directions for the dosage are correct.

Hopefully, as professionals get more and better computerized, prescriptions will be printed and not hand-written. My own cursive is illegible so I can't make any jokes about that. You can, I'm sure, remember when all personal notes had to be hand-written or you were deemed not fit to have tea with the queen. I used to type my notes and letters, always adding an apology or excuse, like "please excuse the typed note, I broke my fingers when I fell off my motorcycle."

Sleep (or Lack Thereof)

Getting a good night's sleep is essential for maintaining your overall health and strengthening your memory banks. If we knew of a sure-fire way of assuring you and ourselves a good night's sleep every night without pills, we would all be very happy campers. The last time I can remember being able to sleep at a moment's notice either in bed, standing up against a wall, sitting at the dinner table with my face in the soup – anywhere – was when I had a baby with colic who slept for about 20 minutes out of every 24 hours.

We have tried all the suggestions, singly and together, and sometimes they work and other times – hah, good luck. Darkened room, keep a small night light on, regular hours, comfortable temperature, not eating too close to bedtime, eating a tiny snack just before bedtime, keeping the room quiet, keeping the TV on, not reading in bed, reading in bed, and what works best for me, not getting all bent out of shape about it. If I can lie quietly thinking nice things like eating a dish of vanilla ice cream with sprinkles on it and actually losing a pound instead of gaining, my pulse slows down, my heart rate slows down and I reap the benefit of resting. Afternoon naps are good, but I'm sure you have already discovered that on your own.

One of the reasons you will not sleep through the night like a teenager is the need to visit the bathroom at least once, if not more so. Every time the air conditioner clicks on in the summer or the heater in winter and wakes you up, light sleeper that you are, you automatically get up to go to the bathroom. As you approach the threshold and have a visual of the toilet (moving quickly to avoid leakage), you try to erase that image from your mind and substitute, instead, a picture of yourself climbing diligently up a mountain or sitting beneath a baobab tree in some exotic land. You want to envision yourself anywhere but on that threshold. Sometimes you succeed. Sometimes you don't. What to do? Adult pull-ups shipped discretely is one option, but who wants to go to sleep in padded panties? Some innovative people simply buy a stack of washrags and clutch them in the appropriate spot to avoid dripping. Then there are the prescription medications with all their advertised side effects. At any rate, unless you go the medication route, book a private room when traveling to avoid unseemly comments about your manner of handling this delicate situation.

Skin – Take Care of Your Largest Organ

Respect the power of the sun. Malignant melanoma is no fun. I know because I've had it and it came from being unprotected from the sun all of my life. Mine was diagnosed early and removed, and I avoid excessive sun exposure like I would avoid the plague. Be aware that it can grow in places on your body that are not exposed, like between your toes or, as mine did, under my arm. Now THAT summer was definitely "not a day at the beach." I bought three extra large black T shirts and lived

49

in them all summer (the wound leaks, in case you're wondering why black shirts). One shirt was on my body, one shirt was in the laundry and one shirt was in a drawer.

Inspect yourselves carefully in a mirror or, when you go for your medical checkups, make sure your doctor looks at the places where you can't see, like your back and on your scalp. If you see a strange growth, go to a dermatologist to look at it. That's how I saved my own life.

I learned how to dress my wound without throwing up, but was not happy about the hole in my arm large enough to put a ping pong ball into. If the spot had been more visible to the public, I would have gotten a skin graft, but when I asked my physician friend M. if it would eventually fill in, he assured me it would. What he didn't tell me -and I figured out for myself - is that it fills in with FAT! Like I need more fat!

Nutrition

Obviously you could devote a whole book to this subject as it pertains to the elderly. Unfortunately, the studies can be very confusing. One proves the importance of potassium, which is readily available in bananas, dried apricots, beets, white potatoes, etc. Another study proves those same foods should be used very sparingly because of their high sugar content. Another study proves that red meat is too high in "bad" cholesterol and we don't ever have to eat it by simply substituting legumes. Other studies prove that it's a good source of protein and potassium. See what I mean? We are also told that dairy is an excellent source of protein and calcium. Other studies show that we should drink no milk, substituting rice or almond milk, because it actually leaches the calcium out of the bones and causes mucus to form, and we don't want that, do we?

How about the study that says pasta has no nutritional value and immediately turns into bad simple sugar? Contrast that with my own study that proves pasta is the ultimate "comfort" food, especially when eaten with creamed spinach, which is full of dangerous salt and bad dairy.

I do feel pretty sure, however, that the advice we received from instructors at Canyon Ranch Spa in the Berkshire Mountains in Massachusetts was reliable:
1. *Maintain a healthy weight.*
2. *Aim for optimal blood sugar, cholesterol and blood pressure levels (i.e., if you go overboard on the creamed spinach, your body will tell you).*
3. *Exercise daily. "Idle feet are the devil's workshop." Did I get that right? Never lose sight of your goal, which should be Lulu Lemon workout clothes without being the laughing stock of your Pilates class. (In this case, the mirror will tell you if you've gone overboard on the creamed spinach.)*

A word or three about vitamins: keep swallowing them. I'm not here to give you a prescription, and this is NOT medical advice, I'm just sharing my own experience with you. My fish oil pill is so big that sometimes I gag on it. I won't throw away the ones I still have, but I'll keep size in mind when it's time to replenish. The smaller the better. I'm still trying to evaluate the efficacy of the glucosamine chondroitin. Those devils are huge and you have to take two. I don't mind the baby aspirin, the 1000 units of D and the 500 of C that I swallow. I can down all three in one gulp. Of course there's the multi and calcium with magnesium. I'm also phasing out the vitamins that have all kinds of other ingredients. What we learned at Canyon Ranch was "If you can't pronounce the ingredient, don't ingest it." There are vitamins out there that are relatively pure. I'm going to phase them in little by little. I also find that a dose or two of psyllium helps with elimination. In old age, it's important to keep regular and all the above ingredients help.

I again turn to Dr. James Gaeta for advice on swallowing pills:
- *Drink a little water before you put the pill in your mouth to wet down the inside of your mouth, then take the pill with more water.*
- *Put the pill in the middle of your tongue or towards the front, not farther back and position oval pills length-wise. Tilt your head forward, not backward.*
- *Try drinking carbonated water. Sometimes that washes down more easily.*
- *If the pill is to be taken with food, try chewing up a bit of food, pop in the pill and swallow it with the bit of food. First try relaxing with a couple of slow, deep breaths.*
- *NOTE: Do not crush or chew a time-release pill. You would get the full dose that way and it could be too potent taken all at once.*

One more note on vitamins (and anything else that comes in pill-form): you have to be a cat burglar to break into some of these bottles. Are they child-proof or are they seniors-with-arthritis-in-their-hands proof? Some pharmacists are now making non-childproof bottles available but not all. For those that don't, I keep bottle caps from previous bottles and pry the insides of the caps out with a screwdriver. That leaves regular screw caps, which I save in a drawer. When I go for refills on my vitamins or meds, I ask the person behind the counter to open the bottle for me, and I replace the lid with one that I brought from my hand-dandy little gizmo drawer. Then you make it child-proof by putting the bottle on the top shelf.

12 ANTI-AGING STRATEGIES

At least once a week, a lengthy article appears in the newspaper about anti-aging. The "Boomers," many of them vocal, educated, intelligent and liberated from the accepted restraints of our generation and certainly the generations before us, have decided to live longer and look better. Youth has been glamorized.

Our concept of a workout was marching around in our "gym suits." They were one-piece affairs – ours were blue – with elastic bloomer pants and our names self-embroidered over the pocket. Does that make some of you smile? Today's gyms are filled with machines with names like reformer, cadillac, elliptical and treadmill, and these people are WORKING, not marching around.

Our beginners' make-up was Tangee Natural and our hair was tamed with water and bobby pins. Today's marketing of hair and makeup products is brilliant. The colors are eye-catching and names include descriptive adjectives like herbal, fortifying, cellular, rejuvenating, flexible hold, etc.

Marketing research firms project that anti-aging products will be a $114 billion-plus industry in this country by 2015. I spelled *that because I don't know how to write a billion in numbers. It sounds more like the national debt. By some estimates, 35- to 50-year-olds are spending $20 billion a year on plastic surgery and non-surgery skin treatments alone.*

The National Institute on Aging advises consumers to be skeptical and on guard for possible scams involving purported anti-aging products. No treatments have been proven to slow or reverse the aging process, so if someone is promising they can do that, they're most likely trying to take your money and run with it.

There are some seemingly magical pills out there for joint pain, stiffness, and muscle pain. I took one a few years ago when it first came on the market. I could not believe how wonderful I felt. I remembered what it felt like to be young and spry. I ran up and down the stairs like a teenager – until my esophagus said in a very clear message to my brain, stop taking this pill before I (my esophagus that is) completely rot away. I listened to my esophagus and stopped. You probably know what I'm going to say next. The FDA took that pill off the market because of the dangerous side-effects.

Speaking of the FDA, although there is relatively little protection for the consumer, government agencies do crack down on flagrantly false claims. And now Consumer Reports has jumped into the fray, testing cosmetics using optical devices and other scientific methods to assess products. The results show that the effectiveness of even the best products is limited. When there are wrinkle reductions, they are slight. Even the best performers reduce the average depth of wrinkles by less than 10% and that is barely visible to the naked eye.

While we have yet to discover the Fountain of Youth, there are a few factors that determine how long we live. Some we have no control over, like having good genes. We can pick a mate but we can't pick our parents. It helps to be female, but again, we are who we are.

It also helps to be rich. As F. Scott Fitzgerald wrote in The Great Gatsby, *"The rich are different from you and me." They have greater access to benefits, healthcare, good neighborhoods and longer vacations. In the U.S., the National Institutes of Health documented that high-income men live about four years longer than lower-income men. However, women in the high-income bracket only live an average of one year longer than women in the lowest bracket.*

Live in the right place. These states report the longest life spans: Hawaii, Minnesota, Utah, Colorado, Massachusetts, New Hampshire, Iowa, North Dakota, Rhode Island, California.

We don't want to scare all of you nice folks from the Deep South, but the following states have the shortest life spans: Mississippi, Louisiana, Alabama, South Carolina, West Virginia, Tennessee, Oklahoma, Arkansas, Kentucky, Georgia.

Get married. Married people live longer than single people. It appears that when wives die, their husbands lose the protective effect of marriage, but when husbands die, their wives retain it.

Stay in school. A study conducted in North Carolina several years ago showed that people with 12 or more years of schooling have a life expectancy between 2.4 and 3.9 years longer than people with less education.

13 EXERCISE

Exercise could also be viewed as an anti-aging strategy, or at least a way of feeling better as you age. You might think that you hate it but if you make it a habit, it gets better and better. It can get so good that when you get a cold and can't exercise, you feel deprived and yes, it does help your reflexes.

My preferred way of exercising is simply walking. Maybe it's not as beneficial as performing squats holding eight pound weights or spending an hour sweating at the local gym, or moving gracefully in Pilates classes, but walking is something I want to be able to do until the day I depart this earth. Besides, moving along on the boardwalk or the beach accompanied by the panorama of the sky and the sea is spiritually uplifting, an added benefit. True, I have to keep muttering to myself, "heel, toe, lift your feet! squeeze your shoulder blades and pull up your core," but when I remember the days after my broken hip when I had to literally haul myself along, hand over hand, hanging onto the railing, I am ever so grateful and happy to be upright and perpendicular to the terrain. Sadly, even when I feel like I'm moving at a rapid pace, everyone else seems to pass me by. But no matter. I am enthralled by the ever changing views of the sea and sky. One day the ocean is a mass of chiseled grey blocks which glint silver in the hazy light. At times the cobalt sea is spread over with glitter and the foam of the depleted waves slowly frolics off toward shore, clapping and twisting along the way. If I'm out toward late afternoon the lowering sun burns a deep rich red just over the horizon, and when I retrace my steps to go back home, there's a different view entirely. Now the strip of blue sea is overlaid with a golden glow which turns the breaking waves a deep amber color. Depending on where you walk, there are different sights to intrigue you. Seek them out.

Alternatively you might want to turn exercise into a social event, attending classes at the local gym or community center. At our community center, they call it "seniorcize." There is Edith, just turned 90, huffing and puffing with as much gusto as the best of us. In the back sits Bill, who walked in with two canes. Someone was happy to get him his chair, his weights, his band, his ball. We laugh and joke as Maryann or Carole leads us in routines or dances. It's better than sitting in the green leather recliner. Get up and moving. That's the answer.

C., who teaches our pilates class on Wednesday nights, is long and lean with a Modigliani neck. A former ballet dancer, she ends our session with a routine and marvels at our coordination as we tap tap tap in first position, then move our arms like the birds in Swan Lake. Her delight is contagious. We feel young and beautiful.

Ideally, you should be doing a little of everything – aerobics to get your heart going, weights for strength, core breathing and stretching for flexibility and balance. Don't do this without trained, licensed instructors. Look for a good class and go from studio to studio until you find the one that suits you.

By the way, exercise won't solve the problem of weight loss. After a lifetime of trying I still have to fight the vices I have struggled with since I slid out of the womb. But getting out to class has great social benefits. You will be with people who are also groaning and breathing hard. You will not feel alone.

14 APPEARANCES – ACCEPT YOURSELF BUT DON'T NEGLECT YOURSELF

You are who you are BUT, get a good haircut and get professional help with proper makeup. Those adorable, disgustingly tiny little girls at the makeup counters really do know their stuff. They have been playing at it since they were 8 or 9 and their own bedrooms looked like the entire makeup section of CVS. Dress for your age and figure, which means, forget the short shorts and cover your knees, for Pete's sake.

Let's face it. You hear about the extraordinary cases, the genetic marvels who sail into old age fortified with great genes. But we're just ordinary human beings and I'm here to tell you the unadulterated truth, although you can see it for yourself by taking a hard look in the mirror. Yes, that's you, wrinkles and brown spots galore. No matter what you do, you're still old. So keep it simple. Forget the dramatic eyeliner unless you want to go the nip-and-tuck route. What? You want to undergo anesthesia and risk more declining mental functions?

If you want a shot of Botox for your granddaughter's wedding and the groom's grandmother is youthful looking and attractive, then go for it, but unless you are an anchor woman on T.V., don't depend on it. Whatever it is you're trying to cover up will fall down anyway. Save your money and concentrate on attitude. A nice smile would be super.

I have a friend who lives in New York. Realizing that she was getting old, she had stopped coloring her hair and started wearing comfortable clothing. One day someone took her for a bag lady and offered her small change. "That's it," she exclaimed, "I'm going shopping!" Now people look at her with respect.

Go shopping indeed. Be glad you are still interested in clothes. Wear what suits you. Wear stylish clothes at all times--even work-out clothes should be attractive. I recall first noticing that many of my hair stylist's elderly clientele come in, week and after week, with their caretakers and canes, dressed to the nines, in sharp contrast to my faded exercise clothes. I am determined to heed my own advice and show up next week in a matching outfit, clean sneakers and makeup.

It took years to overcome my schizophrenia about shopping. My brother once confided in me he had the same problem. We came from a household where our mother was very frugal and our father was openhanded. We would take pleasure in buying, then go home and worry about it. Don't do that. It's not healthy.

Shopping can be therapeutic if you buy less and get good quality. Try for sales. Don't go "bag lady." That only looks good on Annie Hall so don't use it as an excuse to cover up any flaws in your no-longer-svelte figure. You can dress for your age and still be stylish. Remember what I said earlier about the short shorts? I haven't changed my mind.

Guys, you're not off the hook here. If you are like the men in my family, you probably think that everything you need is available on the computer and you will never have to go into a clothing store again. If there's any possibility that the item is wrong for you, call the company and ask for a "consultant" to help you. Most of the big-name companies have them. Usually female, they love to explain and suggest, and can be very helpful. You too, ladies — when in doubt, pick up the phone. And don't lie to them. If your hips are 56" around, tell them the truth.

Shall we talk about how nice it is not to have to shave your legs anymore? Oops, I forgot, it's growing under my nose now and it's called a mustache. Have you noticed that it's no easier for a man? Their hair is being "transplanted" from the top of the pate to the nose and ears. Not a pretty sight, guys. Talk to your barbers.

ODE TO THE RUBBER TREE

Oh, how I love thee
My stretchable waist
Without that elastic
I'd be in disgrace.
My buttons would pop
I'd fall out of my top
And everyone would say
I had terrible taste.

15 FINANCES AND ESTATE PLANNING

If you have been going to a financial planner every few years, you have probably discovered that the sage investment advice offered in year one differs significantly from the reality when you revisit the strategy a mere few years later. The laws change. The amount of money you need to live changes. Your life circumstances change.

Our first consultant told us to buy "second to die" insurance. This policy would enable the kids to pay off any expenses upon our death without having to sell off stocks or bonds at an inauspicious time. The idea was that the initial payments (and they were high) would last a few years, then the interest from and added value of our holdings would take over and we wouldn't have to fork over any more out-of-pocket money. That was all well and good except that the market didn't do so well, our holdings went down in value, and we had to keep paying those large annual insurance bills until we decided to let the policy lapse altogether. As we stopped paying thousands of dollars annually on the policy, we realized that we didn't have to worry so much about the kids' inheritance (if there would be any). Whatever they got was gravy as far as their incomes were concerned. If they had to pay taxes or sell off holdings, let them. In the meantime I'd try to get rid of any encumbrances, like the few acres of farmland we owned.

The plan to gift grandchildren was promoted by our second financial adviser. He didn't take into account the fact that the money the grands received would interfere with their ability to get financial aid. Besides, as the years passed, the money we had put away no longer seemed like such a large amount. In fact, we would probably need it as we advanced in age. The following year we were strongly advised to adopt a 529 plan, a state sponsored college savings plan that invested money like a mutual fund and allowed it to grow tax free. This promise would no longer be viable after 2010. Glad we didn't take that plan, as it is now 2011. As I said, the laws change under your feet as you amble along the road to financial savvy for your estate. We ignored that advice in favor of consulting with a teacher of finance who wasn't trying to sell us anything and who balanced our portfolio to avoid the ups and downs of the market as much as possible. I'm very happy with this fellow. He's more worried about me than about my grands.

In general, I'd say be cautious about giving away cash. No reliable adviser will tell you what to do in that regard. I say use it to enjoy yourselves with your children and grandchildren. Spend your money on trips with them to Europe, on a cruise or on visits to a spa. Those experiences that bind you together are the best big financial plans.

Be sure to keep your important papers in one accessible place. I have a small filing cabinet next to my desk with everything in alphabetical, labeled folders, but keep in mind that I'm a bit obsessive. My family would question the word "bit" substituting "very," but they're over-reacting.

Finally, write out a letter which, in New Jersey, is called a 3B-311. (I'm sure there are equivalents in other states.) It doesn't have to be notarized or witnessed and keep it with your Last Will and Testament, Power of Attorney and Health Care Directive (commonly called a living will). Date it, sign it and list all of your valuable and/or sentimental goodies and to whom they shall be given. "Aunt Griselda's gold bracelet to cousin Godiva Saliva. Uncle Quasimodo's silver tie clip to my great niece Laurinda Melinda, etc. If your cousin Godiva Saliva dies first, cross off her name and substitute my best friend Sasha Natasha.

16 COMPUTERS AND OTHER ELECTRONIC DEVICES

You knew we would have to tackle this eventually. When computers first hit the market, I bought a used HP and even if I had been a computer technician, this old machine would have sent me near the edge. Before we even start, yes, you must learn computerese. Start by going to a reputable store and get something reliable and simple like a Dell. That would be like buying a Honda. Then follow these simple steps:

1. *Understand that when you push a wrong button, it's highly unlikely that you will break the machine. Study the keyboard, study the simplified, consolidated instructions, get a 10-year-old to show you where everything is and memorize the "escape" key.*
2. *Practice using the mouse by playing solitaire and Minesweeper.*
3. *Start typing.*
4. *Keep repeating this mantra - "It will take two months to become even minimally proficient so stay cool and don't panic."*

Pretty soon you will wonder how you managed without it. You will, however, always have a love-hate relationship when it goes on the fritz. Just save everything, sign off, turn off, leave it alone for 20 or 30 minutes and reboot. If that doesn't work, call in a pro. Most computers have the life expectancy of a ferret. When you get to that point, hard-copy everything and go back to the store for a new one.

We cannot stress enough that the cell phone is an absolute necessity. The latest models let you take photos, send e-mails, look things up on Google, and play about 5000 games. They can do everything except walk the dog or make dinner. Be prepared for future phones that will both walk the dog and prepare dinner.

In the meantime, if you are not into all of that, you must have a cell phone that will make calls, receive calls and have the capacity to store numbers. If you have teenagers in the family, learn to text-message or you will never hear from them. Keep the phone on and in your pocket at all times. Charge it every night in a charger that you can reach from your pillow. Keep it on the seat next to you in the car. Do as I say and not as I do. My phone will ring while I'm driving and it's in the deep pocket in my jeans under my shirt, under my sweater, under my zipped-up jacket, under my seat belt. I then pull over, unbuckle, unzip, lift sweater, lift shirt, dig in deep pocket and see that I have missed a call from some blasted telemarketer who wants to sell me a new phone.

The Kindle is nice, but not necessary.
The iphone? The ipad?
Don't ask us. We already told you that we're 81 and 82.

17 WHERE, OH WHERE TO LIVE

When you are suddenly left as the only occupant of your house which originally held three kids, two cats, a dog, your spouse and you, here are some choices:

1. *Stay where you are for one year and then decide – that's what the experts advise.*
2. *Stay until you are taken out feet first.*
3. *Get the heck out of there now while you still have the strength and go into a condo with all of the benefits and uh, hmmm, some other stuff….*

Benefits:

- *Doorman and desk clerk for security and convenience*
- *Everything on one level and reached by elevator*
- *Garage attendant to babysit your car*
- *Someone is available to screw in a light bulb, fetch a painter, do carpentry*
- *Not isolated from other humans*

Uh, hummm:

- *Every head swivels as you walk through the lobby. Your business is their business*
- *You have to dress to get the mail.*
- *Smells - broccoli and fish, for example - taste better than they smell in your own kitchen. Multiply that by the number of units in the building.*
- *You will be mostly with old people. If you want to see an old person, look in the mirror.*
- *You have to tip the garage guy every time you take the car out. In comes the car, out comes the palm; If you take your car out six times, you will tip six times so factor that into your budget.*
- *Someone's window is leaking, but yours is not. You have to share the cost anyway.*

That was just about houses but how about location? Move to another city to be near children? Move to get out of the snow? Rent first, then decide.

No matter where you live, you may eventually have need of home health services. If so, you will be among the 12 million people in the U.S. receiving those services, enabling them to stay out of nursing homes, according to a report by the National Association for Home Care and Hospice. But more and more states are cutting back on those services as their budget deficits deepen. Let's hope this trend reverses so we don't have to go back to the way we coped years ago with three generations living in the same household.

Still, if you manage to live into your nineties you might consider a "mother-in-law suite." When I heard this new addition to our English language, it sounded to me like something out of Hansel and Gretel or Cinderella. Ugh, meddling mother-in-law, mean step-mother? It isn't that at all. Building an addition onto an adult child's house to accommodate an aging parent and still give everyone their needed privacy and independence can be a viable solution. These additions are also known as granny flats or accessory dwellings and builders across the country are getting an increasing number of requests for these add-ons.

A spokesperson from AARP reported that about 3.5 million American households last year included adult "kids" and their parents and this number will rise as the country ages and the baby boomers begin to retire. A two-car garage can be converted to a bedroom, bathroom, and kitchenette, with a separate entrance and doors to accommodate wheelchairs. This conversion is, of course, cheaper than an addition involving major renovations.

Of course it doesn't always work. The property has to be large enough to accommodate this, the parent has to be reasonably self-sufficient, and getting back to Cinderella, all the parties involved have to be cooperative, and able to get along well with each other. Everyone has to take turns cleaning the cinders out of the hearth.

19 TRAVELING

How many exercises do you have to perform each morning just to haul yourself out of the aisle seat in a plane? Thirty reps daily--sit, stand, sit stand, sit stand. In fact, you should stand up at least once an hour while traveling by plane, just to keep from stiffening up (although the attendants would prefer to have you strapped into your seat so they can push those annoying carts up and down the aisles). My bad knees and the hip I broke two years ago make this an ordeal for me, and I see other seniors who have just as much trouble as I do. Then I see some with huge beer bellies who leap up out of the chair like gazelles in the forest. We all age differently and have different infirmities. In order to travel, you have to be able to go up and down stairs and to move at a pace. It's not always easy and you're on your own. To travel you have to keep at it-- moving, doing aerobic exercises, going up and down steps, and forcing yourselves out of the recliner to walk a half hour daily just to maintain mobility.

However, all the exercise in the world will not prepare you for certain trips. The days when you could climb the entrance to Mont St. Michel without huffing and puffing are in the past. At this point, there are many places that you will simply never visit on your own. Recognize that your possibilities have contracted. You will go wherever your friends or your kids can accompany you. By the way, sharing exotic experiences is a great way to bond with children and grandchildren. On these trips they take care of you, appreciate your company, share their tapas with you in Barcelona, and laugh at your jokes as you pick up the dinner checks. But don't forget to get yourself a single room.

Getting around Closer to Home

Check the local papers, pamphlets, and even the brochures taped on supermarket windows for fully planned and escorted day or weekend trips. They can be reasonably priced and you may be thrown in with a jolly group of people. Grouchy people would probably not be attracted to this sort of entertainment. They're too, um, well, grouchy.

If you don't drive, call your local city or county for information on senior citizen's vans and buses for schedules to markets and malls. They're usually driven by good citizen volunteers. There are also drivers for hire when your transportation needs extend beyond the local mall. I'm talking about navigating down the East Coast to visit grandkids, getting to an airport, or maneuvering through bumper to bumper New York traffic to get to a museum. Relatively young but retired people have turned this service into a thriving business that they offer for a reasonable fee. Our driver J. is a retired firefighter and we love him and he loves us.

Speaking of cars, they will give away your age every time. Go for a walk with your teenage grandson and he can ID every car in every driveway. Not only that, but he can tell you who lives there, how much money they have and how old they are. For example, old men drive Mercury sedans and old ladies drive

Honda Accords. Old men wanting to feel young drive smallish convertibles and old ladies wanting to feel safe will drive a Lexus van. Stuff like that. Volvos can go in any direction and pick-up trucks often belong to youngish to middle-aged handymen. If you are not into mechanical things, want reliability, and don't care about image, go Japanese.

20 ATTITUDE IS EVERYTHING

My husband always admonished me that I tended to focus on the negative. I must strive to see events bright as the beautiful harvest moon. I will maintain my independence. I will keep a positive attitude even if it means mumbling those directions to myself as I take a walk.

One way to take control of your feelings is to take all of those expensive tests, if only to eliminate obsessive worries. During the period following my husband's death, I had multiple physical symptoms. It was only after taking the tests and learning the truth that I was able to calm down. It turned out that my shortness of breath was not due to a blood clot in the lungs after my hip surgery. It must have been due to anxiety. The pains I obsessed over, which I (and my physicians) attributed to diverticulitis, to blood clots, to tumors all turned out to be induced by focusing on every ache and pain. I see that the series of physical ailments were really the result of a preoccupation with fear of death. The fact that I worked like a demon to gain strength, to walk without a cane, to exercise, do Pilates, get acupuncture, all pointed to the fact that I wanted to live. Once the tests were over and the results negative, I stopped thinking about all the dire possibilities. The truth helped me develop a more positive attitude.

Here are some other ideas for changing your attitude:

When conversing with our peers, let's try for a ten-minute limit for complaining. Whining is not allowed. An occasional moan is OK. You may say, "Oy vey" because that is not English. Should we answer complaints with advice? No, but we might nod slightly and murmur, "I know, I know" or, if it goes on after ten minutes, "I KNOW already!"

Block the word "guilt" from your vocabulary: If you've done nothing intentionally wrong, mean or inconsiderate, forget you know that word. People use guilt as a weapon. You should neither use it on others nor accept it when it's tried on you. It can be subtle so recognize it and don't fall prey to it.

By the way, there is a difference between regret and guilt. I'm sorry that I left behind in my old house the poster on the wall that my father bought for me when I was a little girl. I regret it, but I'm not beating myself up with guilt over it. I regret that I didn't ask him enough questions about his childhood because I was too young to appreciate what he had to say and he probably would have enjoyed talking about that. I regret it, but I'm not beating myself up with guilt over that either.

Be assertive, not flirtatious. (Remember, you are no longer cute.) The following conversation illustrates this approach:

Me: Excuse me, Mr. 6'4" heavily bearded and completely covered with tattoos driver of this 50 ton truck. Do you think you can move up the street a bit so that you're not parked in front of my house?

Stare-down commences between driver and 5' 1" Mrs. 81-year-old, who is getting a stiff neck from looking up so high. Driver snarls, stomps back to truck, slams door and belches away. Victory for the little old lady. Polite, soft-spoken, determined, assertive demeanor is the key and if you can manage it without hurting yourself, cross your arms in front of your chest while you are speaking, but for crying out loud, don't try to be cute.

Don't think that because you're older, you don't have to censor yourselves. Don't for a minute believe that you are now entitled to say and do anything you want because you have "earned" that entitlement. You may be a little feisty, but not cute (see paragraph above) and bang your cane if you must, but only against the floor and not someone's shins. You are not entitled to be rude, discourteous, indiscreet, presumptuous or arbitrary. Reinstall your "filter," people.

Get rid of useless compulsions. Stop compulsively worrying about a dinner you're hosting, about house and car insurance bills you have to pay, about your overspending on a large catered event. Those concerns loom large at 3 a.m., but when dawn breaks, you'll see they are not that important.

Worrying is just one component of a larger problem, stress. The following are some ideas for keeping that monster at bay.

Mindfulness: paying attention on purpose. Be willing to experience what is happening now. When we are present with our experience, rather than caught up in our constant thinking, there is a greater serenity and peace of mind. So stay in the moment.

Be a better friend to yourself. Don't stop trying to do your best, but be accepting of your own feelings and attributes, whether they fall short of your expectations or not. Permit yourself lapses into despair or whatever other emotions arise, and don't be ashamed of them. Accept aberrations in your behavior, excuse yourself, suffer your peculiarities, suspend judgment.

Be grateful. "Gratitude is a positive response to the reality of our dependence on other people," said my friend's father, a college president. "Gratitude says so eloquently that I know something of who I am because I know I need other people." Yes, there's a lot for us to complain about at this stage of the game. But I have children who love me, a son who tells me their house is open for me whenever I want company. I have sufficient money, a lovely home. All of these things sustain me on a daily basis.

Cultivate friends of all ages. Go to the supermarket for take-out and gather around someone's dinner table and talk about current events, philosophy and music. Did John McCain screw up his presidential bid by taking on Sarah Palin? Is circumcision mutilation or a health benefit? Were the abstract impressionists really angry or just liberated? Can Sarah Palin really see Russia from her window?

Hobbies:

- *Gardening can be beneficial to the spirit but bending over can be beneficial to your physical therapist.*
- *Photography - excellent. When you can't remember where you were, look at the picture.*
- *Music - avoid playing the tuba, harp, or bass viol. Too heavy.*

- *Board games, card games, crossword puzzles - all good.*
- *Volley ball, tennis, running - all bad unless you're in exceptional shape.*
- *Horseback polo - bad. Water polo – good.*

Last but not least, don't sweat the small stuff. As we are reminded every day when we look in the mirror, we are rolling towards the last stop on this ride, so we can't waste time on non-productive, energy-sucking attitudes. If you think old, you are old. If you think young, you're still old, but as Mark Twain said, "It's mind over matter. If you don't mind, it doesn't matter."

So, get out of your green recliner, and make the best of the rest of your journey.

Alia Sayegh and Lois Wallen were both born and still live at the southern New Jersey shore near Atlantic City. Their friendship spans over 75 years, but they have both traveled many miles in different directions over that time period.

Following her undergraduate studies at New York University, Alia traveled abroad and worked for four years in an Israeli kibbutz. She returned to the United States and worked in the Atlantic City School District for thirty-four years, first as French teacher, then as Supervisor of Fine and Industrial Arts and finally as District Supervisor of Foreign Languages and English as a Second Language. During that time, she earned her Master's in Education and Doctorate in Romance Languages at the University of Pennsylvania. Alia has three children and four grandchildren.

Lois Wallen earned her business degree from Temple University, which she put to use as office manager and bookkeeper for her husband's law practice. In addition to running the practice and raising two children, she trained as a docent at the Noyes Museum of Art in Oceanville, NJ, where she still enjoys taking tour groups through the galleries.

The authors have set up a blog where they will continue publishing their thoughts on aging - gracefully and otherwise. Readers are welcome to add their own comments. Please join the discussion at www.TheGreenRecliner.wordpress.com.

19042798R00050

Made in the USA
Charleston, SC
04 May 2013